Contents

TROUBLESHOOTING METHODOLOGY ....

WELCOME

Hello, and welcome to my new presentation of the CompTIA 2013 Edition of A+ self-training. Now, I'm C.V.Conner and I'm very glad to be with you and I'm going to take you through the technologies that are going to be tested on the latest CompTIA exams. Now, CompTIA does a real good job of updating their exams every three years or so, and it's been three years already. The 2013 Edition's out at the time of this writing, this book will cover that and be good for several years coming, and what I'm going to do is take you through the basics of the technologies that you need to be aware of and the new technologies that have been added on these 2013 Edition exams to help get you prepared for the A Plus Exams. Now, A+ is one of the most widely recognized computer certifications in the world and it really helps you to have this on your resume. So, with that, let's jump into the course and get started. Thanks for purchasing this book committing to make a better life for yourself and/or your family here.

Now before we actually get started with our A+ Self-Training course, let me give you some course objectives so that we kind of understand the playing field here. The purpose of this book, what I'd like to do for this course, is help you prepare for your actual certification exams, and that includes exams 220-801 and 220-802, all the way up thru the next three years or so. Remember where I stated above that CompTIA changes their exams about every three years. So if you're finishing up this course anytime between 2013 and 2017 then this book should still be applicable for your self-training. But let me give you my book disclaimer here, and make sure you understand this. First of all, batteries are not included with this course. In other words, you cannot just sit and look at this book and just kind of let, you know, eight and half, nine hours of information blow by and think that you're going to pass this exam. You will have to energize yourself. You will have to grab onto this information and you're not just trying to memorize data here. You really need to gain an understanding of how this stuff is working and how this stuff kind of correlate to other things that are happening in the computer as well, so you'll have to exercise some brain power here, and I'm not trying to imply that you won't, but just understand that trying to memorize as much data that's included in this book is probably not going to happen. So you'll actually need to learn this stuff and save your ability to memorize for the two (2) study guides that you're going to get after completing this book. You need to have an understanding of that. Also, your mileage may vary.

You've heard this one before. But depending on where you're coming to this course from determines a lot of how much you're going to take from this course and understand, two different people can use this course and see different things jump out at them. Now, if you're brand new to the whole A+ objectives and certification and you haven't had a whole lot of hands-on with PCs, I'm trying to build a course for you and give you enough background information but if any of it seems over your head at all then I would suggest that you supplement what you see here with some other reading and some exercises, some hands-on outside this, and if you've been here a while and you've been working on PCs a while and you're just kind of brushing up when you go take this thing, then just kind of skim through here and watch for just those little tidbits that you tend to forget. For example, we don't work with the different types of RAM every day. We don't necessarily work with motherboard form factors every day, and so those kinds of things, use it as a refresher to kind of remember what you need to just memorize and that sort of thing. So anyway, this course is going to be a little bit different from any other course that I've written, and so it could be different things to different people. Now, if you print out, and as a matter of fact, the CompTIA A+ Essentials Objectives for 220-801 and 220-802 is on the CompTIA website. What I want you to notice right off the bat though, and I'll mention this a couple of times throughout the course - I'm not following those objectives in order because they don't necessarily go in an order that is conducive to learning things in a layered approach and building on top of one piece of knowledge on another. They're just listing the topics you need to be aware of. So, I'm not going to go in the order of those objectives, however, that is a great study sheet. When you complete this course, I would print out those objectives and I would go point by point through that list and look at something and when it says DDR you're like, I know what DDR is. Here's just a little bit about it. Fine. Go to the next one and it talks about, I don't know, EMI. And you're like, OK, I know what EMI is. I'm cool with that, got it.

Static Charges - all that kind of stuff. As long as it makes sense to you you're fine but when you see something in that list and you're like, I'm really not sure. I don't remember. There's a red flag. Go read up, study on that, go back and watch a YouTube video, get out on the Internet and read, and that sort of thing.

Also, understand, it is not possible - there is so much information that you could be tested on here. If you're new to this do not just complete this course and go try to pass this exam. If you're brand new and this is the first certification exam you've ever taken, this is your first hands-on really with A+ and that sort of thing, I would highly recommend that you go back to Amazon or Barnes & Noble's and buy the two study-guides that I wrote to accompany this course. There you will be introduced to the exact questions and answers that are going to be on the exam, and if you memorize the study-guide and combined with what you've learned in this course, passing your exams should be a real breeze to you.

To be an A+ technician there's a lot to know and more than just knowing the data you really need to understand how it all fits together because a lot of times the memory that we put in our machine is going to affect how our video performs, how the computer itself performs, and we just need to understand how these pieces fit together to really get to where we need to go and to be able to answer some of the questions on the exam and in the real world. This course and the two study-guides are designed to get you there in about 21 days! So that's the objectives here - to get you up to speed, regardless of where you're starting from, and for some of you guys, give you a launching point to continue your learning and kind of brush it up, and for others to kind of help you refresh and get ready to pass these exams. So anyway, let's get started and I hope you enjoy it.

INTRODUCTION

Now as we jump into the course, let me go over the course structure with you and explain a couple of things. First of all, we're going to jump on PC Basics and just kind of cover some of the basic things that you'll see on the exam historically, ESD, EMI, RFI, those kinds of things. We'll talk about the various Connections on the PC, and let me point out here; I'll say this in a couple of places in the course. If you look at the CompTIA printed Objectives for the A+ Essentials Exam I'm not going in the order that they list these objectives in because they're just kind of listing them to let you know what you need to study. They don't have them in any kind of chronological order that helps, especially for those of you who are kind of new to this, to kind of build an understanding in a logical way, so I'll deviate from their structure on their Objectives, but I will cover a vast amount of that stuff if not all of it. So, anyway, we'll jump on the Connections and then we'll move to Memory.

We'll talk about things like the types of RAM, types of DRAM, RAM characteristics, that sort of thing. From there we will jump on Processors. We'll talk about popular Processors, Speed Buses, Registers, Cache Memory, Co-Processors, on and on and on and so we'll cover all that, get you up to speed. We'll talk about Hyper threading, a popular question on the exam. But then we'll jump on the BIOS and the CMOS and then from there go to the Expansion Buses on the Motherboard. I'll talk about what those are, what you do with them, what you need to know, obviously, for the exam on those kinds of things. And then the Motherboard and those irritating Form Factors that you have to know for these exams - that's memorization but we'll get on to that. Then we'll jump on to Power Supplies, some of the items that they tend to test on, and then we'll jump into Hard Drives. Quite a bit of information will be here, we'll talk about some of the Hard Drive basics, some of the storage terminology you need to know, the types of hard drives and how they've evolved. Solid state Storage, the various other types of Storage Media - optical, magnetic and so forth.

Then we'll talk just a little bit about Operating Systems and this is one place where I will deviate from their outline. I'm not going to go entirely through what they show on their objectives. And what I will strongly suggest is you have the Operating System on your PC, look at their objectives and just go chase some of that stuff down and play with it. Get hands-on with that Operating System and you will be fine. But we'll cover quite a lot of data on the Operating System to show you the things that historically have been there on the exams. Then we'll talk about some Video and Audio things that you tend to see. Some of the video and display choices, video cards, resolution, some audio basics to get you past the questions. Then, of course, Printers. Everybody's favorite!

There's still questioning on laser printer steps, we'll talk about that. Networking is another popular topic. You need to know it real world and on the exam, and so we'll talk about just some basic Networking, what it is, cabling, hub, switches, routers, topologies. Then we'll hit some TCP/IP basics. Then jump on the Internet, just a few things that you tend to see on this exam about the Internet. Then everybody's favorite, Security, and then we'll close it out talking about some Soft Skills. So, as you can see, we're going to cover a lot of information and this is probably going to be a little bit longer a course than what you normally see on these types of courses, but there's a lot of information here, so just kind of wanted you to know where we're going and keep in mind, I'm going to do this in an order so that I can kind of lay a foundation for you and build on each level so that they all kind of build on each other and make sense. As I stated earlier, by popular demand, this book is going to be a bit different from any other book I've written on computer training. A lot of people have written to me asking to change my format more suited for someone who knows absolutely nothing at all about computers, and this book is the result of those requests. And last but not least, I write the same way that I talk, so if you can get past my country-boy existence, and just focus on the information I'm giving you, you're going to be just fine. So, let's get at it.

COMPTIA A+ CERTIFICATION BASICS

First, I want to go over just some basic aspects of the A+ Certification to help you understand exactly why you're going to inflict this amount of work and study on yourself, and so the basic question for most people is: exactly why would I want to pursue A+ Certification? Now you've probably already asked yourself this question and come to the conclusion or you wouldn't be reading this book. But I want to give you some foundational things to think about as you go through here because the more seriously you take the process and the outcome, the easier it is to learn this information and the more it kind of sticks in your brain, if you will. The first point that I want to make here is that the A Plus Certification is the industry standard for computer support technicians.

And the bottom line with this certification is that it demonstrates knowledge and competence that you have in the installation of basic computer systems, the maintenance of those systems, networking those computers together, security aspects of everything that's going on with the computer, and then troubleshooting computers to understand why they're not functioning the way they were expected to. Now the absolute bottom line with this whole idea of A Plus Certification is a big one for you, and this is the aspect of A+ Certification in that it provides human resources, or HR, with an extremely valuable acronym, and that is CYA and, of course, CYA means Cover Your Anatomy.

Now, there's an old story, an old saying out there in American business that says you can't go wrong by hiring IBM, so if I'm put in charge of some big computer project in my company and I go out and hire IBM and then later the project just doesn't turn out like we thought or the technology aspects of that project don't quite come up to the standards that we had hoped for, I'm always going to say, when it comes to, you know, taking care of myself, hey look, guys. I hired IBM. I mean, what else can I do? Now had I hired my brother-in-law to come in and he kind of knows a lot about computers and things went wrong, now I'm in trouble. But I hired IBM. The same thing. When a human resource person sees this A+ Certification on your resume they know that they're getting someone who has done quite a bit of study, they have a lot of hands-on experience, and they know what's going on with the computer and it just makes their job safer for them. Another reason for A+ Certification is that it's part of the certification track for other very well respected industry certifications.

Microsoft, Hewlett Packard, Cisco, and Novell are just four of the big ones, and for example, with some of Microsoft's technical certifications the fact that you have an A+ Certification counts as some of their basic prerequisite exams and what this means to you in English and in dollars is that by passing the A+ Certification track you have one less test to take on the Microsoft side. And so when you get ready to jump in, say, to a Microsoft technical exam track or certification, you've already got one out of the way just by holding A Plus. And another thing that has happened is, a lot of companies have now made A+ Certification a requirement for all their service technicians, and we're talking about, especially here in the U.S., some of our largest corporations and even if you work for these people and you weren't A+ Certified when you got there, they will require you to achieve this. Now for most companies, especially the large ones, they advertise to the end users that, hey, all of our technicians are A+ Certified, and often you have to be in possession of the A+ Certification before you can ever get hired at those companies.

Now the A+ Certification structure was simplified in 2009, so now you simply have to pass two exams and that is, the CompTIA A+ Essentials Exam, (I normally recommend that you do the Essentials Exam first) - we'll get into that more later in the course as to why - and then you need to pass the CompTIA A+ Practical Application Exam. So, my suggestion to you is to do Essentials first and then Practical Application. If you currently hold the A+ Certification on the 2006 or 2009 Objective, good news. You only have to take one exam and, of course you have to pass that exam but you only have to sit through this one time and for that you'll be taking the CompTIA A+ 2012 Bridge Exam. So, that's just some very basic facts, ideas, helpful pieces of useless information maybe for you in working on A+ and just the basics about the Certification and what you can expect for it. Now, you're not going to walk in an HR office and say, I have A+ Certification, and they're just going to go nuts and start throwing six figure salaries at you, but this is the way to get your foot in the door in the IT industry and it is a way to show human resource people that you have the basic skills to provide quality work for them and you're also greatly reducing the risk that they take in bringing you on and sending you through the training processes for their company and how they work and so forth. So, that's just a little bit about the basics on A+ Certification.

THE EXAM / TESTING BASICS

Now let's concentrate just a little bit on some testing basics on the A+ Certification and specifically let's talk about what are the requirements or the prerequisites for taking the A+ Exams. Interestingly enough there are no prerequisites necessary – or at least not yet. The bottom line is, if you can go schedule an exam and pay the 168 dollars, which is what it cost at the time that we're producing this course, and they tend to hold these prices for long periods of time, but for 168 bucks, if you can schedule that, pay the money, you can go sit the exam, try to answer it, try to pass it.

Now, CompTIA recommends, and I strongly agree with them, that you need at least 500 hours of hands-on experience with PCs to be able to successfully navigate this exam. Now, those 500 hours doesn't mean that you've been working for a company for that amount of time on computers. There are a lot of people who switch. They're in an administrative role, or they're in, you know, the mail room or something, and they want to get into IT and so they will go take an A+ Exam. You don't have to have 500 hours in the office there. You can play with these things at home. I always recommend people volunteer. That is what I did at the beginning of my IT career. If you're a computer nerd at heart and you've been playing and messing around with your PC at home and you've gotten real comfortable with a lot of the technologies and operations, go volunteer for your church or civic organization. Non-profits always need someone to help them, especially with computers because out there in the consulting world it usually gets really hard for them to pay a lot of the prices for a couple of reasons. Number one, they tend to be kind of cheap because they have to be because they're working in tight budgets and then, number two, it's hard to lay out large amounts of money on things that aren't what they're about and so those places are great. Public libraries, just anything like that, someone that'll let you get your hands on and it's a very non-confrontational environment because, hey, I'm working for free, OK, so give me a break here and let me figure this thing out. But you can get a lot of real good experience there, but roughly you should have about 500 hours of hands-on experience with a computer.

Now when you go sit these exams and we've already talked about that, you have the Essentials Exam and the Practical Application. That Essentials Exam is going to focus on technical understanding and communication with the end user, but it is going to really drill in on technical understanding so you're going to have to be prepared and be familiar with things like motherboards, CPUs, USB drives, different types of hard drives and the technical aspects of that. That is why I always recommend people take the Essentials Exam first because the Practical Application Exam is going to ask you a lot of the same type questions about exactly the same technologies that you saw on the Essentials Exam except that the Practical Application Exam's going to come from a little different perspective and it is going to focus on troubleshooting and it's going to test your knowledge of the tools that you need to use to resolve certain problems. And so, the Practical Application kind of becomes OK, so you passed Essentials and you've got the technical stuff down, now do you know how to put the technical pieces together to troubleshoot, find a problem, and then use the correct tools to solve those problems? So that's how the two tests kind of interrelate. Now the big question you get from a lot of people, I get them in live tours on A+ for new people – truck drivers and so forth. I did a class one time with 12 truck drivers in the class; they're all trying to get A+. First question: how tough are these exams? Are they tough? Is it hard to pass? The answer: yes and let me qualify that. You are expected to know a lot of different technologies here and you'll have to study.

You're also going to expect to understand a wide array of functionalities of the technologies and go ahead and write this down: do not intimidate yourself here.

There are very few people out there who are up to speed on all the topics that you're going to get on this exam, especially to be knowledgeable enough about them and to be up to speed enough to go pass the exams. And I know very few people who can just walk in and pass the A+ Exam because there are just parts of the PC that we don't deal with every day and we have to go back and refresh ourselves. So, just mark that down. I have over a dozen professional computer certifications, and I couldn't just walk in tomorrow and pass the newest A+ exam.

Now the other half of that answer of course is no, the exams really aren't that tough if you have that hands-on experience that I mentioned above, and you use my study-guides. If you have that hands-on experience and if you prepare for the exam by reminding yourself, well, you know what, there is quite a few different types of hard drives and I don't really remember, you know, how those connectors look and which ones are faster or slower, so you will have to prepare and memorize a few things. And another good thing that makes this exam not so tough, there are no trick questions. Now, if you ask someone who's ever taken a Microsoft Advanced Certification Exam and I've sat through quite a few of those, there are some seriously tricky questions on those exams and you'll get double negatives and triple negatives and all sorts of things. You don't see that on the A+.

They're very straightforward. They're not trying to trip you up, they're asking you straightforward questions and if you have studied and you have hands-on experience you will walk away and say, that really wasn't that tough an exam.

Now, all of your relatives and anybody who's not had a whole lot of hands-on on computers will think that you're some sort of, you know, wild maniac rocket scientist type person, but you're going to know a lot about a computer by the time you get through studying for and passing the A+ Exam. So that's just some of the things to keep in mind. Do not get intimidated here. Do not get psyched out by how much you have to learn. If you buy a book to study A+, the book's going to be thick. If you look at the length of this course it's long, but take it step by step. Not a problem. Get hands-on. That's the basics.

TAKING THE ACTUAL EXAM – Part 1

Obviously, one of the major parts of A+ Certification is being able to take the A+ Exam successfully, meaning that you pass the thing and you obtain the Certification and so in this section, which is going to be Taking the A+ Exams Part 1, I'm going to begin to step you through how to prepare for and pass these exams. And this is going to be a two-parter in and of itself, so in Part 1 we'll just kind of get started. First of all, you need to study. Now this goes without saying but it is amazing how many people really try to go take these exams when they haven't adequately studied. You'll hear me harp on that and complain about that all the way through this course and warn you about that. The next thing, once you have adequately studied, and let me back up there just a moment. By studying I mean read some books, get hands-on - make sure you hear those words get hands-on with a PC. A self-study course like this that you're looking at right now is an excellent resource but let me warn you, you will not read a single book, watch a video series, a course like this, or go sit in a class for a week and leave there and go pass the exam. Most people simply will not do that. They will have to get hands-on and then, another great tool is to use my study-guides, and if you've never seen these things, they are developed to mimic the A+ Exam. Most of the study guides out there is not going to be the same questions you get on the A+ Exam because that violates CompTIA's agreement, but in my study guides you will see many of the exact same questions that will be on your exam because I have not signed a CompTIA agreement. Make sure you use those. Pay close attention to the questions that you miss. Use these things as an indicator, as a weakness guide if you will. It's like, man, they're always confusing me on the types of memory - DDR, and PC100, and all that kind of stuff. Obviously that's something you need to go learn. Memorizing the answers on my study guides and impressing your spouse or your neighbors or your in-laws with the fact that you can make 98 percent every time on the exam, they will be impressed, however that's not preparing for the actual job. The exam is going to question your technical knowledge and your ability to recognize when that technical knowledge applies, OK, so the secret here is know why a correct answer is correct and know why the incorrect answers are incorrect. So you're not just going to take the exams from my study-guides, you're actually going to study this book first OK? Now, schedule the exam. This is another one people trip up on. You need to schedule the exam and make that a drop dead date that I'm going to be ready. Life is what it is.

Don't kid yourself about it. If I tell you I'm going to call you sometime and we're going to have a meeting about this great new project guess what? You'll have to call me back in about eight months and say, remember me? But if we set a schedule and it's in my Outlook and it's on my phone and it's screeching at me that, you know, you've got this appointment coming up in a week, in three days, in two days, in one day, I will prepare for that meeting. The same thing with this. Schedule the exam, let it hang over you, let it haunt you. You'll get ready for it. When you're ready to schedule the exam you're going to go to pearsonvue.com, or to prometric.com, either one, and this will let you search out for an examination location near your home or business or wherever, and you can choose one, you can schedule the date, the time, and you can pay the money. At the time of this writing, like I said, it's $168.00 per exam. That stays pretty standard. They generally don't go up a whole lot. So you schedule your exam, you study, you do your practice exams, and then you arrive at least 15 minutes early. You do not want to arrive late. You don't want to be frantically driving across town making gestures at everybody, running red lights because, for whatever reason, you're running late. Make sure that you time it so you hit the center 15 minutes early. I like to go in, any time I take an exam - I've taken hundreds of these things - is go in, sit down and go over my little list of things that I needed to memorize. Types of RAM, you know, distances on network cables, that sort of thing. Anything that you have to memorize, I'm just going to sit down in the lobby there and go over and refresh my brain on it just a couple of minutes before I actually get in there. So then you will identify yourself.

Now, keep in mind, you can't take cell phones, pencils, paper, notepads, backpacks - you can't take any of that stuff into the exam so leave them in the car. When you get in there and you're getting ready to start the exam you're going to have a little, a piece of paper and a pen that they provide you, that way they know that you haven't done any tricks by impressing answers into the thing or anything like that. And what

I want you to do is sit down at the desk and before you kick off that exam by putting in your Social Security number of whatever into that computer, write down your troublesome memorization items. If you've had trouble remembering types of memory, write them down. Get all that stuff down on that sheet of paper. Now that becomes a reference object for you during the actual exam.

Then kick off the exam. You're going to get 90 questions. You're going to have 90 minutes to answer them. You have plenty of time, don't worry about it.

Now once you kick off that exam there are some things that you absolutely positively, definitely need to do and I'm going to stop this section right here. This will be the end of Part 1, take a little break and then join me in Part 2 and we will finish up how to take the A+ Exams.

TAKING THE ACTUAL EXAM – Part 2

Welcome to Part 2 of Taking the A+ Exams, and I really should have added the word Successfully on there but let's just continue where we left off in Part 1.

You have begun the exam. Here's what I want you to do. Read each question completely and do it twice, and do it slowly. Make sure you understand what the question is asking and make sure you don't psyche yourself out. Now, this is going to be something that you're just going to have to be able to determine when you're in the test. Most of these tests you can mark a question as skipping it and then you can come back to it later. So here's what I want you to do. Sit down and start the exam. You just got there, you're nervous, you paid 168 dollars, your spouse, your in-laws all know that you're coming, and your mother-in-law's just waiting for the chance to prove that she was right about you all along. You all know those pressures. So I want you to sit down, look at the first question. If you don't positively, absolutely, no doubt know the answer to that question do the little check box, skip the question, go to the next one. Now just make sure that it's the type test that you can come back to the question, but if you see a thing up there where you can mark it and come back to it, do that. Do about six or seven questions that way and, trust me, at some point you're going to see one that says: Does the word computer have a U in it? And you're like, I know that one. And you check it. You won't get a question that simple but you know where I'm headed here. Once you see a couple of questions that you know, magically your nerves start to settle down and suddenly you go from being this confused worried character to you are now "Joe Computer" and you've got it, and all the things that you've learned start just flowing out of your consciousness and you know the answers to these things, or you'll know a lot more of them. At some point you're going to go through the test and you've answered the ones that you just know and a lot of times those will trigger other things that you couldn't remember.

But what happens when I get to a question when I just don't have a clue? Here's what you do. Disqualify the answers that are clearly incorrect. If you have four choices a lot of time one of those choices is simply ridiculous and you can easily spot that one.

Another one is not right, you're pretty sure it's not right, and the other two are possibilities. So at least get it down to a 50-50 and then make your best guess. Then what I want you to do is make a mental note about this particular topic or technology because if, for some strange reason, you don't pass this test this may be the reason why and you want to come back and study this later.

And, also there's an even better reason. You're going to need to know this in the real world. You can't go to an interview and say, well, when I don't know the answer I make my best guess. No. In the real world you can go research it, but it would be better if you understood it, OK, so make sure that you keep in mind you're doing this for a real world situation.

Now, at some point you're going to get to where it's time to end the exam. You will usually have 15, 20 30 minutes left over. It just doesn't take 90 minutes to answer these questions. If, as long as, you haven't spent too much time on a question you're not sure about - they ask you a question about a hard drive type - don't sit and stare at that screen for 45 minutes waiting for osmosis to give you the answer. Mark it and go to the next one. Then go through all the questions, answer the ones you know, then go back through the questions, look at the ones you marked and see if anything has jogged it loose and use all of your remaining time reviewing the ones you weren't sure of, alright? Very easy to do. However, as you're going back through them, do not psyche yourself out and start changing answers on the questions that you knew. A lot of times our first inclination is the right one. Now here's what's going to happen. You're going to finish, it's going to say in the exam calculate my score and you're going to do that. It's going to sit there and click and hum to torture you for what seems like forever. It'll pop up your score and tell you whether you passed or not. If you did not pass join the club. Do you hear me? Everybody fails these exams at one point or another. It doesn't mean you're stupid. It doesn't mean you have no business being here. It just means you're human, OK, and you didn't pass the exam. Go to the front desk, get your score sheet from the lady.

I want you to take the score sheet from her or him. And if you did not pass sit right down in the lobby, flip it over, borrow a pen and write down everything that you can remember on that test that confused you. That's your new study sheet. Then you can retake the exam. You can reschedule it, pay another 168 dollars (that's the hard part)- as quickly as you would like for the second try. I would suggest get in there in two or three days, take it over. Keep in mind, you've been studying and a lot of this is in your brain but you just couldn't recall it during the exam.

So get back in there quickly, kind of study up on the areas that tripped you up and confused you, get the second one. Now I really want you to try and memorize as much as possible from my study guide for this book because as I said it contains many of the exact questions that you will see on your exam. And the reason I write study guides is because it makes testing easier and faster, and it does not give you a shortcut to becoming an A+ certified technician who isn't qualified, as many would lead you to believe. No, you self-trained first so a study guide of the questions and answers just assist you in proving what you know.

If you fail the exam a second time you now have to wait two weeks, 14 calendar days, to schedule the third attempt. Now it gets harder across two weeks to remember all this stuff, so take my advice and get my study guide(s). Now, if you read your score and you passed that means you made at least a 675 on Essentials or a 700 on Practical Application. I want you to join the club. Just like people fail these things people pass these things. Go to the front desk, get your score sheet just like before.

Take the score home, keep it in a safe place. That is the only real proof you have that you passed this exam, and provide a copy to your employer. Ask them to put it in your human resources file. This is candy when somebody else in the company looks for you or might pull your file. Now you'll say, it don't work that way in our company. It doesn't right now, but if they hire a new HR person that doesn't know anybody and they pull your file and guess what, there's paperwork in there. You know, Bob has A+, James didn't. Let's go with Bob. OK? Trust me. That happens. If you go through these steps that I've laid out here in taking the A+ Exams, Part 1 and Part 2, it will be infinitely easier on you and trust me you will get passed these exams. So, go back through them, do what I said. Trust me here. This should help tremendously.

COMPTIA TESTING TOPICS TO EXPECT

Let's take a look at the Test Topics and these are the areas that you need to be aware of that they're going to question you on the A+ Exams and so I just want to work through these and show you what to expect. In this course I'm preparing you for both of the A+ exams, and the Objectives are published on CompTIA's website, and I'm just going to briefly reproduce these for you.

But, you need to look through these and a great way to know if you're prepared for this course is to look over the Objectives and just look at the things and look at every item and think, yeah, I know what that is. Yes, I can do a little one-sentence explanation of that. Anything that doesn't pop right into your head as something you're aware of then that's something you probably need to go read about, get some hands-on with, that sort of thing. So just know that on a hundred question exam, 27 percent of the questions are going to deal with Hardware in some way, so roughly, if we do the third grade math here, 27 of your 100 questions will involve Hardware. Twenty percent of your questions will involve Troubleshooting, Repair, and Maintenance and you can already see how overlap's going to occur. One question may have to do with the technicality of Hardware, you know, how far it'll reach, who knows what - how many megahertz it's running at, what that means.

The other troubleshooting question could have something to do with a hardware piece that's malfunctioning, so again, you can see the cross-talk here. Operating System and Software will comprise 20 percent, or roughly 20 of the questions. You'll get maybe 15 questions on Networking. Now, keep in mind in each one of these instances the Objectives break these down. I didn't list those here because it would have been 20 more pages of stuff to sleep by, but for example, in Networking you don't have to be a Cisco Certified guru to pass this thing. On the Networking portion you just have to know roughly what TCP/IP is, some general troubleshooting things with TCP/IP, so in each one of these I'm not going to drill real deep, but they are going to expect you to be aware of certain aspects and I'll help you with that.

Security is going to comprise about 8 percent of this course. Again, you don't have to be a Firewall expert but you do need to understand some basic security functionalities, especially in your Operating System and software. And then just Operational Procedures, and we'll talk about that. That is really Soft Skills - how to deal with the people that are asking for assistance and so forth. So, that's where you're headed, and that's what you're going to be looking at on both these exams and so what we're going to do now with the rest of the course is start to step through here and talk about the technologies and functionalities in each one of these and get you up to speed and help get you ready to go pass this A+ certification.

PERSONAL COMPUTER BASICS

  Let's talk about some PC Basics. Now this is foundational for getting started preparing for an A+ Exam and that is exactly to kind of lay the groundwork for what a PC is and what its basic functionalities are, and it really comes down to four things. Any computer device, be it a PC, any kind of hand-held device, tablet PC, telephone - any of that stuff - is all involved with these four things: Input of data, Processing of that data, the Output of that data, and the Storage of that data sometimes. Sometimes we want to store it, sometimes we don't. And obviously when we get into all of this each four of these can be broken out into further subdivided aspects and these kind of overlay the Objectives for the A+ course. Now, let's look at a picture here.

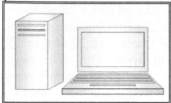

  I've got the PC and so the first step that happens is Input. Now that's going to come through a keyboard, a mouse, say some sort of biometric device that reads retinal scans or thumbprints or fingerprints or something along that way, but some way we need to input or talk to the computer, so that's the first step, Inputting data, instructions, information into the PC.

The next step is going to be Processing.

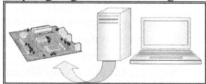

  Once we send data into the PC via the mouse, the keyboard, a microphone, anything like that, it's going to have to be handled by the motherboard, by the CPU, the Processor in other words. Maybe some peripheral devices that are plugged into the PC. If I'm using a microphone then that data's going to get onto the motherboard and be processed via a microphone cable that's plugged into an audio card that's stuck onto the motherboard that is exposed out the rear of the PC. So, anything that we input is going to have to somehow be processed and so we need to understand that parts and pieces of the processing on the motherboard and then a couple of other places, and how those can work, how different types of processing pieces make us have a faster more efficient PC, and how those things can go wrong and we need to repair them. Then once we've processed our data then we need to Output it in some fashion.

  Now, I've put a printer as the next picture here because let's just assume that we've typed something into Word and so we've input some data into an application and the data was processed onto the Word document by the software and now we need to print it out. Keep in mind that Output could be sending it across the Internet to someone, it could be placing it somewhere else in a workflow, and then the last one is Storage, and obviously we need to save that to a disk. Now, I've put a hard disk on here but understand, this could be an SD card, some sort of Flash media, a USB drive. It could be in the Cloud on kind of a remote disk somewhere, but anytime you touch the PC, anything that you do or are concerned with it, it's going to fall into one of these four categories: Input, Processing, Output, and Storage, and that is where we begin when we start to look at getting ready for A+ certification.

ESD/EMI/RFI

One of the topics that I can absolutely, positively guarantee that you will see on the A+ Exam(s) is a question about ESD. ESD is another one of those three-letter acronyms to avoid. CIA, FBI - those kinds of people that we generally don't want to be involved with those folks unless we're getting paid by them, OK? ESD is Electrostatic Discharge. We're talking about static electricity here and it occurs naturally, meaning you will have to deal with this and it can cause you tremendous problems. What exactly is ESD? It is simply the passing of a static electrical charge from one object to another and this occurs quite naturally when two objects have different amounts of static electricity and they come into contact with one another. Physics being what it is, some sort of natural law's applying here, electricity will always try to even itself out. This is why when you walk across carpet on a cold, dry day and you touch a door knob you get that little shock. When you put on a sweater that has a different static charge than you and then you touch something then you get that little shock. This occurs most often in a dry, cool environment.

Notice that's the second time I've said that in this course. That usually is part of a question on the exam. It's a dry, cold day in Mississippi and Billy has been working on a PC. Everything looks fine but he came in from lunch, he walked across the carpet, he put the cover on the machine and now he notices the memory's not behaving correctly. Well, Billy probably touched the PC and created a static discharge and probably fried his memory. Keep in mind, humans can't feel a static shock that's under 3,000 volts. Notice I said static shock, OK?

Computer components can be damaged with as little as 10 volts, so it is very, very easy to touch a computer or a computer part and have a static electrical discharge and seriously damage that particular part or that computer. Now how do we avoid this? One of the ways - watch for this on the exam - is by using an anti-static wrist strap, and this is where we're going to first discharge any static difference from us and the computer on a piece of metal somewhere, or we can also touch the power supply on the computer because that should be grounded if the computer's plugged in.

But anyway, we're going to discharge and then we're going to put this wrist strap around our wrist and then with that alligator clip connect it to metal on the computer and this will serve to keep me connected to the PC and it will keep the static potential between me and the PC equal and there won't be any jumps in voltage and I won't damage the PC.

Another thing that I can do is use an anti-static mat to avoid that, and this is something we simply roll out on the floor in front of our work bench and then we can attach that particular alligator clip to a ground and this will, when we step on it, it will discharge from us out to the ground and then we can keep things safe that way. Another way that we avoid electrostatic discharge, especially when we're dealing with parts of PCs is with an anti-static bag,

and you've seen these little foil-looking plastic bags that parts come in, and the reason they do that is that if you put your components in that static bag then the bag sheds the static electricity and keeps it away from the component inside, and so any time you order a part and you open the box you'll notice it's in that bag. Keep that bag. Don't throw it away because when you need to remove a part from a PC and store it you need to put it in one of these bags to prevent an ESD situation with it. There is another way, and there is a workaround on ESD. I've actually already mentioned it. Watch for this on the exam and that is, when you walk up to a PC to work on it touch the power supply first. You want to make sure that you keep the static charge between you and the PC the same, the power supply's already built to deal with this and it won't pass it onto the rest of the PC as readily so touch it, and then touch it repeatedly as you work on the PC. And a lot of people will say never take, always have one hand on the PC, never take one of your hands off the PC while you're working. That's easy to say, hard to do, so you really want to use a wrist strap, a mat, or again, touch the power supply first and keep touching it repeatedly. This is going to keep you at the same static charge as that PC. And then, one last little warning here: always unplug a PC before you work on it.

It's not a good idea to work on a machine that has a lot of electricity moving through it - just a safety thing there. Watch for that on the exam as well. So, that's ESD. It's Electrostatic Discharge. We just simply don't want to fry the computer with this difference in electricity that builds up and again, I'll mention it one more time, this happens in cool, low humidity environments, so obviously you could put a humidifier in your workshop and not let the humidity drop too far in there and that, again, will help you avoid ESD.

THE TECHNICIAN'S TOOLKIT

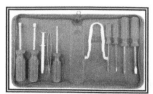

The Tech Toolkit is one of those items on the A+ Exam that you're not going to be asked directly about it per se, but you may have questions that involve different tools that are in it and so I want to bring these to your attention and this is just a good review of some of the things that you will need in the PC support technician or repair technician's world.

The basic tools that you're going to need as a tech or as an A+ Certified person is going to be something very similar to this. Now this is the most simplistic, and you can see these things, you can buy them in electronics stores, you can find them sometimes in some of the hardware stores, the Home Depots, the Lowes, those sorts of things, but I wanted to point out some of the tools that you're going to see in here that you need to be aware of and understand what they're talking about if they mention them on the exam, now, Phillips-head screwdrivers, that's pretty straightforward and we're talking about these little four-

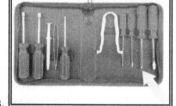

slotted head screwdrivers.

Phillips-heads are pretty basic. Look them up if you don't know what they are. Now, Star-headed

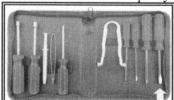

Torx wrenches, and you will just hear these normally called Torx wrenches, and some people will misspell these and call it torque, t-o-r-q-u-e that has to do with engine ratings, but it's really Torx, and these have this little six-sided star type arrangement as you see here, and you can get them in multiple sizes and some computer manufacturers use these things on different parts of the assembly and so you'll have to have those. A lot of people confuse these with Phillips-head but understand Phillips-head screwdrivers will not work with these things, especially if they've been tightened at all. So that's a Torx wrench.

Flat-head screwdriver's pretty straightforward. It's this little guy right here.

It's just a flat screwdriver and a lot of these kits will have multiple sizes of these flat and Phillips-head screwdrivers. The next thing is the IC Extractor.

Now this is the one that you need to really understand on the exam because as you'll notice with the IC Extractor, when we're trying to remove certain parts from the motherboard we want to be very careful that we don't grab them with our fingers and start pulling on them because a lot of times your fat fingers are in some very tight places and you will inadvertently knock something else loose or break something and then you've just got a bad situation. If you'll notice this IC Extractor is really a set of kind of basic tweezers but it has these small hooks on the end so that we can reach under the various parts to pull them off the motherboard and we only then are applying pressure to that particular part. So when you hear IC Extractor, that is the tool that they're referring to.

Next on our Toolkit, now this thing is incredibly useful. I pull this thing out of my computer toolkit and use it around the house all the time for all sorts of things, but notice the three-pronged parts retriever, and that's a tongue-twister by the way, and some people just call it the grabber, and so we'll go with that here. The grabber.

This is really like a hypodermic needle.
It's spring loaded and as you depress this end, these little guys pop out. Now, depending on your model, you may have three of these little prongs or four of them. They're little wires. This is great when you're trying to remove something or you're working on a computer and you drop a little screw or a very small part and it falls onto the motherboard especially. Again, we don't want to reach down there with our greasy fingers and try to, you know, wedge them in between parts and grab a little screw or something that we've dropped. We want to use things like this to reach around on that motherboard and grab things because we only grab what we need and we don't knock other parts loose.

And then, of course, you have a set a tweezers, and these are just basic what I would call bathroom tweezers that you see in medicine cabinets, and you'll use these for all sorts of things.

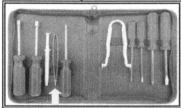

Again, to pick things up, to hold things in place and so forth, as you work. A good basic Tech Toolkit is fundamental for you and on the A+ Exam you will see questions that involve your knowledge of what these particular tools are and how you would use them.

EXTERNAL CONNECTIONS Part 1

External Connections will, no doubt, be a part of a lot of the questions on your a Plus Exam simply because we have so many connections on PCs now and we use every one of them in different ways and we continue to evolve. It's like every time you buy a PC there's a new connector out there. And what we are starting to see now is more of an adjustment in the way these connections are used, in other words, the way that the manufacturers and the standards people put together to use the various wires and pins in these connections but that's outside A+, just don't go there.

What you need to be aware of is the eight major types of External Connections on a PC and then just understand what they're talking about either by the description that they use in the question or the solution or by the shape, and they can from time to time show you a shape on the exam and they want you to be able to tell them what kind of connection that is. These eight major types of connections are: DIN connections, USB, FireWire, DB, RJ, Audio connections, HDMI connections, and Fiber connections.

Now you don't necessarily have to know what these acronyms mean but you do need to know what these do, kind of what they look like, and where you plug them in, so let's just jump into this.

Now this is going to be a two-part Chapter or section, especially the way I tend to get distracted. I will not get all this done in one section so this is Part 1 of two parts. The first thing you need to watch is the nomenclature that they will use on these things and you will also hear this just destroyed out there in the real world the way we interchange these various terms and so I want to kind of clear this up.

Now this is the technical definition of these but again, you will see people absolutely destroy these terminologies out there as they interchange them. Plugs, Ports, Jacks, and Connections. Now a Plug is a part that has something that is inserted into something and a plug is something on the end of a cable generally. A Port is what the plug gets inserted into. A Port is the hole, OK, it is the hole on the back of the computer that takes a cable being plugged into it. A Jack is also another word for a Port.

Now usually a Jack is used to refer to a network connection or a telephone connection and that kind of came out of the telecom world. And then a Connector is a generic term for a Plug or a Port. And actually, a Connector is the hard plastic part on the end of the cable that determines the layout of the pins, but as long as you can understand what these are talking about this will help you move through some of the questions on the exam. Now let's just jump into some of these.

A DIN connection - and don't worry about what DIN stands for, it's a German name, they won't go there with you; you can look it up if you would like. But, early PCs had a DIN connection and this thing was fairly large and this is what it looked like.

And this was used to connect keyboards and that sort of thing and computers still use these but they use a smaller size and they're called mini-DINS. They look the same way, they're just smaller and we also know them as PS-2 connections, so on the exam you probably will see something about a PS-2 connection and just understand it's a mini-DIN connection and, more importantly, this is what it looks like. No doubt, if you have a desktop PC, if you flip it around and look at the back of it this is how your keyboard and your mouse is connecting and that's the most generally accepted use of that connector.

Now, USB has exploded and taken over the computer world. It provides all kind of magic. You may see this definition Universal Serial Bus, is what USB stands for - and this is really now the most common general-purpose connector for PCs. We hook up thumb drives, we hook up external hard drives, all kind of peripherals, cameras, scanners, printers, all kinds of things go through USB. There are three different sizes and you need to be aware of these as you go into the exam. The first is A, the second is B, and the third is Mini-B. So let's take a look at each one of these.

The advantages of using the USB technology on all of these connections is that it's what we call hot swappable. Watch for that term on the exam. It means that I can just plug it into the computer or unplug it from the computer at any time. I don't have to shut down the computer and reboot it. That seems like an old archaic foreign concept nowadays, but in the early days, probably the first five years that we had PCs, almost any change you made to the PC you had to shut it down and restart it to recognize that change. USB devices also get their power through the USB connection or through the USB cable and this was big when it happened and it's still big. USB devices can also recharge their batteries via the connection and a lot of you folks have cell phones that you can use a USB plug to plug it into your computer, sync it up without looking, those sorts of things, but also it'll recharge the batteries because it has that power pin and that wire running through there. Now, USB-A is probably, to most people, the most common. This is the large flat

connection, just like you see here. It's a rectangle shape and again most common type. And when most people think USB they think this type of connector. USB-B is this small square one with two of the top corners kind of rounded off.

Now this one is usually, you'll find it at the opposite end of a USB-A connector. Now a quick trip to your local Radio Shack or computer store or Best Buy or something you can see all these connectors and I would strongly recommend you go look at them. But, a USB-A connector, a lot of times, will have one of these on the opposite end or it may have another USB-A connector on the opposite end; there's no hard fast rules, but you will never see a USB connector that's a B style on the PC itself. In other words, it'll never be a Port. And we're going to stop this section at this point and allow you to take a small 15 minute break, and then join me in Part 2 and we will continue to discuss External Connections.

EXTERNAL CONNECTIONS Part 2

Welcome to Part 2 of External Connections and in Part 1 we ended right here talking about the USB-B style connector, and I completed that section saying that you will never see this as a Port. Now keep in mind, what I mean by that is you will never see one of these protruding out the back of a PC. You may well see the kind of female version of this as a Port on the PC but you will only see this male version on the end of a cable itself.

So again, keep that in mind and pay attention on the exam that they're not asking for the wrong connections on the wrong ends, and again, what I would suggest you do is, a great way to study this stuff especially on these connectors, is go to Best Buy or if you have Micro Centers, or any of those kind of stores, whatever your large computer-type store is, just go look at the cables that are hanging there. Look at the backs of some of the PCs. If you see a connection, you're not sure what it is, ask one of the techs there, say hey, what is this connection and what's the deal with it? And you can learn a lot that way. So a lot of really cool ways to learn the information for this exam and you can kind of make field trips out of some of it and look and play with some of the cool new technologies.

The last USB connection you need to be aware of is the Mini-B connection and this is what it looks like.

Just make sure that you learn the shapes of these so that you can recognize them on the exam. This is usually used to connect to small devices. You'll see a lot of cell phones using these, a lot of the small external hard drives that we can get now for laptops and our PCs use these. This is basically a manufacturer's choice. This is a standard on the connector and the size and the wires that are running through there, so just make sure that you can recognize this on the exam and know what it is.

Now, FireWire is one of those technologies that hit the market with a big bang a few years ago and it brought some really cool stuff. Now what's interesting about this is that Apple Computer actually trademarked their implementation of the IEEE 1394 standard, so one thing to watch on the exam when they mention FireWire they are talking about IEEE 1394 and if they mention IEEE 1394 they are talking about FireWire. So what Apple did was they basically created this functionality based on those standards and you can see what the connector looks like here.

There is a FireWire and then this is kind of referred to, or some people will call this 9-pin, they'll call it all

kind of things, and they'll call this one a lower number, usually 4-pin, but as you can see, the smaller version of this is really just a little square that has kind of a bump in one side. Very easy to recognize and these have two speeds. You can be running 1394a that runs at 400 megabytes per second, and then 1394b runs at 800 megabytes per second, so just be aware of the differences between these. Just remember B is faster than A and it's 400 and 800.

Now, what's interesting coming down the pike out there, the 1394 standard has now evolved to where they're talking about 1600 and 3200 megabytes per second, but you're just now really seeing 800 start to kind of saturate the market out there. Keep in mind, this was kind of grown or developed out of

Apple's need to move non-linear video editing signals back and forth between computers and hard drives and so forth, and so the whole Apple graphical video world kind of was the impetus for developing FireWire, but this has now kind of migrated over into the Windows-based PC world as well, so you see this all the time, especially in hard drives where they're trying to get a lot of through-put on those cables.

DB sub is kind of the old standard. This kind of connector was back on the first PCs. It's still there in different forms, although you don't see them. It's a slight D shape. Notice if you turn this thing up on its

side it looks like a D.
You'll see them in male and female versions in all kind of places and this was originally used on computers to connect printers and any other serial devices and generally this is a serial connection in a lot of cases. But the bottom line is, these things are being replaced more and more by USB, so it's getting more and more difficult other than a VGA connection that uses the D-sub type layout, you don't see these as much anymore, but again, kind of go to your local computer store and you'll notice really what's falling out of favor out there and what's being overtaken by other standards.

RJ is very simple. We all know about RJ if you've been around computers very long. The RJ-45 is the standard Ethernet connection. You'll see these connections, you'll see the Port for this on laptops, desktops, all kind of Ethernet-based devices, routers switches, all that sort of thing. The small one is the one that they'll trip you up on and this is the telephone connector, and we might not even see those that much anymore but the RJ-11 is what you plugged into the phone jack on the wall and the modular systems that plugged into the phones. Two sizes – very easy to remember: RJ-11 is the telephone line, RJ-45 is the network cable; 45's larger than 11, so just always use that to remember that RJ-45 is the big one and then here's kind of a head-on view of the RJ-45 down here.

And you will usually hear these referred to as Jacks, not Ports, that we plug these into. That's just some terminology that came through from the old telephone world. And these cables, again, were commonly used to connect network cables and phone lines, very easy to remember. And that is the basic External Connections that you need to be aware of and we covered those in both Part 1 and then here in Part 2.

AUDIO CONNECTIONS

Audio Connections are very simple. You will see a question about this on the exam in some form but it won't be a direct question, it's one of these that'll have to be inferred most of the time. To connect audio to the PC you just need to remember that we're going to use a Mini-audio jack and this is called two different things.

It's called a one-eighth inch jack or a 3.5 millimeter jack, and the reason they're calling it a Mini-audio jack, if you've ever been around like professional quality microphones, or PA systems, if you've ever been in a band or been around that whole music scene thing, you've seen these larger versions of this that are like quarter inch, that you'll see on the ends of microphones, on the ends of guitar cables, and so forth, and this is just a smaller version of that. Now you also need to keep in mind, don't get confused, but you have seen 2.5 millimeter jacks on packages, in technical materials, and so forth. Two point five millimeter jacks generally are the ones that are used for headphone connections on cell phones, so don't let them confuse you there because you have seen 2.5 millimeters mentioned in a lot of places. Usually the documentation in your cell phone or when you went to the store to buy a headset for your cell phone, if it was wired. So, here's the bottom line. On audio connections you're going to use these Mini-audio jacks, one-eighth inch or 3.5.

They're going to plug into the sound card into the appropriate Port or the appropriate hole back there, and whether you're plugging in a microphone or headset, or another audio device you're going to use these 3.5 millimeter jacks, and of course, like everything else in electronics there are all kinds of adapters out there that will adapt from a quarter inch down to an eighth and from an eighth or a 3.5 millimeter, both are the same, down to a 2.5 – all those kinds of things.

But make sure you understand about this one-eighth and 3.5 millimeter. Same thing, that's the standard audio connection for a PC.

DISPLAY CONNECTIONS

Display Connections are another topic that you will need to be familiar with generally to be able to answer some of these questions properly on the A Exam, so let's take a look at those. These are pretty straightforward.

When we're talking about Display Connections we're talking about connecting the PC to our monitor or our monitors and a lot of times we have multiple monitors now, but it's very straightforward. Just make sure that you're familiar with these various connections and what they look like and we will, no doubt, dig into some of these a little deeper as we go through different aspects of our course here in different sections. But kind of the standard monitor or display connection for a long time was this guy right

here, the VGA, and this VGA connector, notice it's a D-sub type connector and it's basically a 15-pin. If you notice there's three rows of pins and the middle one's offset, but VGA gives us kind of standard display - we'll talk about resolutions and stuff later. Video Graphics Array is what it's called and it's 15-pin.

DVI is the Digital Video Interface and this is what it looks like and there's a lot of things going on with this connector, but the bottom line is, is that if you understand and recognize this pattern, and notice there's a - this is the female version; there's a male version just with pins in this layout – DVI provides digital interfaces. It gives us clearer picture, higher resolutions, you know, some of these resolutions you see on monitors now, 1920 and all that sort of thing, is coming through DVI.

Now, S-Video is one of these consumer-level video things that was supposed to be really cool and make it very easy. Depending on where you stand, you either like this thing or don't like it. On the professional end of audio-visual these things are kind of laughed at. It's kind of a composite video kind of a thing and it just, it kind of suffers from being kind of the lowest common denominator of a couple of things, but you will still see these connections out there in some places. But for the general, what you're going to see most on the A+ Exam is going to deal with the VGA Connector and the DVI Connector. Now, the next one, the newest, coolest kid on the block with monitor and video is this guy, and this is the

HDMI Connector. Make sure that you are able to recognize this because on the 2013 Objectives you will see this one no doubt. This is the High Definition Multimedia Interface. This is what is introducing the marriage of a lot of other display devices to the computer world because, if you'll notice here, this picture of HDMI Port on the back of a game player, OK, and I don't remember which game player this is. Maybe it's an Xbox, but anyway, the bottom line is, is that HDMI has become a standard for high def multimedia interfaces and you will even see this particular port on a lot of the large, high-def televisions, flat panels and things that you see out there. Again, go to your local Best Buy, whatever your electronics store is, Fry's Electronics, whatever you have in your area in the U.S. I'm not sure what you guys have in other parts of the world but go to your local electronics store and take a look at just the various devices and you will see anything that is display-oriented now you will see this HDMI Interface. This is some really cool stuff. Most of your laptops now that are new have this. Just make sure that you can recognize what it is and then we will get into some links and that sort of thing a little bit later on in various parts of the course.

HDMI, by the way, is one of those things that it would not hurt you one bit to prepare for the A + Exam, just to go out and Google HDMI and just read about it a little bit or go to your local bookstore, grab a book and just kind of dig through it and look at HDMI. Read up and this is right now the cutting edge side of monitor connections so the more you can know about this probably the better it's going to help you both in the real world and on the A+ Exam.

MEMORY

Memory is going to be one of those very basic aspects of the A+ Exam and in this section I just want to kind of lay down some of the very foundational aspects of memory that you need to be aware of and just have it straight in your mind as you go into this exam and you're going to do just fine. The first thing to remember is that there are two types of memory in your computer that you're going to be concerned with on this exam. The first type is going to be Read Only Memory, or ROM and you'll hear it called ROM and you will see it in both of these forms on the exam.

The second type is RAM, Random Access Memory. Now keep in mind that technically Random Access Memory covers any memory that we can write data to and then get it back later on. And we'll talk about that more as we go through here. So let's concentrate on ROM or Read Only Memory here for just a second.

First of all, Read Only Memory is just exactly that. We can only read from it, we can't write to it, so the question becomes well, wait a minute, how did any data get there to start with? Well, the data is loaded by the manufacturer and this is not memory that's designed to be very easily written to and so as a result we can only read from it. Now the real bottom line with this is, is that usually this memory is pre-programmed by the manufacturer and it's placed on the motherboard and the computer uses it in various forms.

Early on, ROM was exactly that. It was just, it was designed, it was put on the board, and to change it you had to change the motherboard. Then we saw the introduction of EPROM, or Erasable Read Only Memory, and Erasable Read Only Memory means that the manufacturer can write to it. In other words, they don't have to actually replace the memory module by unsoldering it from the motherboard and then soldering a new one; the manufacturer could write it but it required a special device using ultraviolet light which really means, in English for all practical purposes that this can't be written to either because it means we have to take our motherboard out, use the ultraviolet light thing and so forth.

What we're dealing with now, most of the time, is EEPROM, Electrically Erasable ROM, or you'll hear the term Flash ROM, and when you hear somebody saying I Flashed the BIOS, or I Flashed some aspect, they're talking about this technically Read Only Memory that the manufacturer will provide you with special software. You can download the software and you can Flash your ROM. You run the software, it has the ability with very specified instructions built just for that P-sub memory hardware if you will, that particular ROM chip, and it will actually go in there and re-write that software for you. But from that point on again, it is Read Only Memory for your functionalities.

Now, Random Access Memory is what we usually think of as memory. It is a place to write data for later retrieval and this is usually the computer's primary working memory. Now here's a term you need to kind of hang on to, RAM is volatile and by volatile we mean it requires constant electrical current to retain the data.

Now you could theoretically make the case that your hard drive is a version of RAM because it's random access. We can write to it, we can read from it, but your hard drive is non-volatile. In other words, we don't have to have power applied to that to retain the data, but it's using magnetics and a whole different deal we won't get into here, but we can turn the power off on our hard drive and it will retain the memory.

RAM is usually what is meant by the word memory. When somebody mentions memory in a PC, when you read how much memory a computer has on the little card at the computer store or on the Internet, whatever, they're usually talking about the RAM memory, this volatile read and write memory that we install in the little slots and it's usually, you know, nowadays we're talking about a gigabyte, two gigabytes, 4 gigabytes of RAM, but that's the basics on memory. As long as you understand these aspects of it you've got a real good foundation for understanding what they're talking about. Now in separate sections in the course we're going to talk about the different types of RAM and then we'll dig a little deeper into D-RAM there, and then we'll talk about some characteristics of RAM and some other things, but here's the foundation. Start here and then we will build.

WHAT IS RAM?

There are a number of different types of RAM that you're going to find in the computer and you may see questions about these on the A+ Exam so let's go through them here and give you the basics that you need to understand.

First of all, there are six types of RAM that could be addressed on the Exam. This is: DRAM, SRAM, CMOS RAM, Shadow RAM, VRAM, and WRAM, or wha-ram you'll hear some people call it. It's kind of bizarre but you will hear those terms out there. First of all, let's talk about DRAM. DRAM is Dynamic RAM. It's the most popular type of memory in use today. We will actually dig into DRAM in some separate areas. The data that's stored in DRAM has to be constantly refreshed and that means the data has to be read from the memory and rewritten back to the memory. There's a lot of different types and again, you can see the section called Types of DRAM and that's probably going to be a couple, maybe three parts, and we will drill into DRAM because you will see this in a concentrated form on the exam.

SRAM is called Static RAM. It's faster than DRAM, it's also more expensive than DRAM. Data stored in SRAM does not have to be refreshed, meaning that we don't have to read the data off of there and then rewrite it. I've already mentioned it's more expensive but we usually use this for that cache memory and in different places in the course here we'll talk about L1 and L2 Cache, and it's very fast and the processor uses it, but that's what that's used for.

CMOS RAM - here's one for the relatives on the holidays if you want to impress somebody. Complementary Metal-Oxide Semiconductor RAM. In English this is the RAM that we use to store configuration information for the computer. This is volatile memory and so to hold this configuration information between shut down periods there you'll see a small battery on the motherboard, to keep a little charge on this particular memory to protect that data. Now this is something that you will see. This is also called Flash RAM by some people, but CMOS RAM is what that is, and just think - let me just back up here, let me just give you one little kind of hint - that when you hear the word CMOS just think battery, OK? CMOS is the one that has the battery and that's the easy way to remember that one.

Shadow RAM. This is the process of copying data from ROM to RAM. Back in a separate section called Memory Basics we talked about what ROM is, Read Only Memory. Read Only Memory is really cool to have because it's like hard coded in there, we can't change it, and during things like the boot process we're going to use that ROM. The issue is, is that that ROM may be slower to read from than RAM is and so during the system boot we're going to shadow that ROM which really means we are going to read the data from the ROM into RAM and then we're going to read the startup data from the RAM. So, in other words, we're just going to create a shadow copy of that into RAM just to use while the boot-up happens because we can read from that RAM faster than from the ROM. This increases our boot-up speed and this is something that Microsoft's been wrestling with. If you've noticed, in Windows XP, the first time we saw that boot-up we were astonished that the machine actually started it fast and gave us our desktop. Windows 7, the same way. You'll notice Windows 7 gets you a really quick desktop most of the time.

VRAM, Video RAM. This is just RAM that's isolated onto a video card, so if you go buy an expensive video card that you add to your PC it's going to have some RAM memory on it. This is dual-ported memory. It can be written to and read from at the same time because obviously, with video, we're having to move a lot of data around. This is specialized memory for that purpose.

WRAM is Window RAM, and this is a modification, a new and improved version of VRAM. This is where the guy yells, wait, don't order yet! There's more. You've got video RAM and then you have 25 percent faster WRAM. The main difference here is the price. Go to your local computer store, look at your video cards. The ones with VRAM are one price, the ones with WRAM promise a whole new life, better looking, more dates, faster service, all that sort of stuff. So, just know WRAM, better version of VRAM, roughly 25 percent faster. That's the types of RAM that you're going to find in your PC. Just be roughly familiar, just like I've presented in this section, about what the differences exist between these different types of RAM and where they're used and you should be fine for getting past the questions on the exam.

TYPES OF DRAM – Part 1

Welcome to Part 1 of Types of DRAM. This is going to be a two-parter because I've got a lot of things to cover here, but since DRAM is the most popular type of memory used in our computers today that will be reflected on the A+ Exam, so let's step through DRAM.

First of all, there are nine types of DRAM and I've got to get something out of my system. I don't know if it hits you this way, but DRAM looks like a misspelled word. It looks like a typo, doesn't it? And I keep waiting for the Spell Checker to grab it and correct it into some word but, that's just one of my pet-pives.

First of all there's Standard DRAM; there's Fast Page Mode, or FPM; there's Extended Data Output, EDO; Burst Extended Data Output, BEDO; Synchronous DRAM - that sounds like a good one, Synchronous DRAM, SDRAM; Rambus DRAM, Double Data Rate, DDR; then there's DDR2; and then, of course, there's DDR3. Now the reason we keep updating these is because we're always trying to get more speed, more efficiency. Nobody wants to wait and so let's dig into this and I want to show you how they're achieving these better efficiencies out of these RAM modules.

Let's start with Standard DRAM. Let's talk about how DRAM is read because this is the basis of how all these enhancements happen. First of all, out there in your memory, your actual RAM memory is laid out, if you could see into that chip you would see something that looks like a grid, like an array for

your developer types out there, and what's happening is the first clock cycle happens and if you go to one of the sections on the Processor we talk about clock cycles and the drummer for the PC and all that, so a clock cycle happens, instructions are sent out, and the first clock cycle sends a row address saying I need the data that's stored at row address 1. The next clock cycle sends a column address, column

1, right, and so it's pointing to here. It sends that. The third cycle reads the data, boom. It says, OK, give me that data that's stored at position 1-1 in this particular memory location.

Now the fourth cycle sends the next row address which happens to still be 1. The fifth cycle sends

a column address which happens to be 2. The sixth cycle reads the data, boom, there it is. Now it took six cycles to read the data in these two locations - that's Standard DRAM.

Fast Page Mode simply saves us a step in those six steps. It does not require a row address because once we have sent a row address, it assumes that we're talking about the same row unless we send it a new

row address, so back to our grid, step 1. The clock cycle sends a row address, row 1. It sends a column address, column 1. The third cycle reads the data, there it is. The fourth cycle does not have to send a row address. The fourth cycle simply sends the next column address which is 2 and the fifth cycle reads the data. We did the same amount of work in five cycles instead of six. Not a tremendous saving, but it did save us a clock cycle. Fewer instructions mean faster response, but again this is all happening millions of times per second so it can be pretty significant for us.

Now let's move on to Extended Data Output, or EDO Memory. You see this stuff plastered all over these laptops and computers in the computer stores, oh, this has EDO, whatever, whatever. And everybody's like, wow, I think I'll get that one, and nobody knows what EDO is - well, not nobody, but most people, your average consumer certainly doesn't. But you do, now, and you can impress your relatives when the holidays get here, OK?

Data can be read from memory using EDO while it's still listening for the next instruction. That means the controller doesn't have to do this, you know, cycle 1 read, cycle 2 writes and so forth, and it doesn't have to keep passing all these locations in separate cycles. It's basically doubling up the instructions on the cycles. You get 10 to 15 percent faster performance than FPM and you see what we're doing here, we're really just finding ways to logically double up on our instructions and on the data that's coming back.

Now, Burst Extended Data Output - next step up. Here's our grid . When one memory block is read, for example, we read from this one, we know where we're headed, right? If we read from this

memory block , what's the chances that whatever was saved here extended into the

contiguous blocks , and we need that too. So the system, when it reads this one just automatically bursts or invades or whatever you want to call it - we'll call it burst because that's the name of the memory functionality here - it bursts into the next two blocks and reads them. It just assumes the next two blocks will be needed. Well, guess what? Usually when it gets back to the processor it says, hey, you know what? I'm glad you grabbed those while you were there because I really can use them. So it's usually correct and it saves, again, a lot of clock cycles here.

Now, I will quote a little Paul Harvey here and give you the rest of the story. This is faster by 50 percent than EDO Memory, however, it's not utilized very often. Why? Because the stuff's moving so fast in a technology standpoint that SDRAM came out and most manufacturers simply skipped over BEDO, or Burst Extended Data Output and went straight to SDRAM and that's what we'll take a look at in Part 2 of Types.

Welcome to Part 2 of Types of DRAM and in Part 2 we will continue right where we dropped off with Part 1 and we were talking about Burst Extended Data Output RAM.

Somebody worked very hard, not many people use this, they went straight to SDRAM, so let's talk about SDRAM. Synchronous DRAM is where someone finally woke up and said, hey, wait a minute, guys! Why don't we just make this memory run at the same speed as the motherboard that's making requests in reading and writing data to and from that memory? Made good sense. So what's happening here is the data in the RAM chip is being refreshed and read at whatever the system speed is on the motherboard.

Really, we're talking about bus speed here. Remember that DRAM memory has to be refreshed. The data has to be read from it and rewritten back to it every so often. Here's the only catch. Your memory speed now has to match the system speed and there's a little caveat here, at least, and so let's talk about that.

If I have a 100 Megahertz motherboard then I need to use SDRAM that's running at 100 Megahertz, so that they will sync up. So the RAM is getting the data from the motherboard at the speed the motherboard's sending it. If the RAM's running slower than the motherboard then our data's going to back up like a traffic jam, we're going to have some problems. So this is why you began to see PC100, 133 and all that stuff out there in the marketplace. Now here's a little oddity that you need to watch for on the exam.

If I'm using Synchronous DRAM, and just remember it's trying to sync up with that drummer on the processor if you will, or on the motherboard, go to some of my processor sections to learn about the drummer and the clocking and so forth.

But memory that's actually faster than the motherboard will work as long as you understand you're paying for something you're not getting. You've got a 100 megahertz motherboard, you can buy 133 megahertz SDRAM and plug it in, the memory will work just fine. The only problem is, is it's willing to go as fast as 133 but it's only getting it at 100 megahertz so basically you've paid for 33 megahertz of performance that you're not getting. That's your call, but just understand it will work like that.

Now, Rambus DRAM or RDRAM is just simply a high-speed version of DRAM. It runs at approximately 800 megahertz. This is really cool, however, the motherboard, the chipset, everybody on the board has to support RDRAM. You can translate that to mean that it's more expensive than SDRAM. As a result, people decided I'll just stick with SDRAM. Then, of course, DDR came out and people said that's even cooler, we'll go with DDR, thank you very much.

DDR - Double Data Rate RAM. Let's talk about this. This now transfers data twice during each clock cycle. Go back to Part 1 of Types of DRAM if you haven't seen it, and look at the example where I'm stepping through what's happening on each clock cycle. This is simply doubling up what's happening on the clock cycles. Now this is usually 184-pin DIMM Module. We're going to talk about DIMM and SODIMMs and stuff in the next section or the section on RAM Characteristics. It may not necessarily be next but you will see a section called RAM Characteristics and we'll talk about the different module layouts. You may also see this in a 200-pin Sodium Module for laptops. Now why all of a sudden are we seeing these pin numbers? You could see those on the exam, so just remember those on these particular pieces of memory.

Now DDR speed is somewhat confusing. Now I know this is going to shock and disillusion you that they would make something like this about your computer confusing, but here's what happened. DDR speed is measured in megahertz but it's labeled as the megahertz times 8 because we're talking bits and bytes, humidity and all that stuff. So PC1600 memory actually runs at 200 megahertz. How do you get there? You take the 1600 in PC1600, divide it by 8, and there's your speed, 200 megahertz. So, PC1600, 1600 divided by 8 means I'm looking at a 200 megahertz speed piece of memory.

DDR2. This is a newer, shinier, faster, better, younger, cooler, more hip version of DDR. You get it in 240-pin modules. It requires less power. It runs at 400 megahertz which means you're looking at PC32 on that label because 32 divided by 8 is 4 (400). Now what's interesting here is that 3200 that runs at 400 megahertz is the same speed as the fastest thing you could get with standard DDR memory, and then we start to push the envelope a little more.

PC4200 runs at 533, if you do the math. PC5300 runs at 666 megahertz, PC6400 runs at 800 megahertz. Now let's jump to DDR3. You know where we're headed, right?

Now this is twice the data rate of DDR2. We just keep milking more functionality, more efficiency out of here. Another 240-pin module. This reduces power requirements by 30 percent. PC3 6400 runs at 800 megahertz. This is also known as DDR3 800. Now this is interesting. You can take the 6400, divide it by 8 and its 800, but you're also starting to see in some of the packaging and labeling, they will now call it DDR3 800. So when you're looking at PC3 6400 it's the same as DDR3 800. Is anybody confused? PC3 85 runs at 1066 megahertz.

It's also known as DDR3 1066. The bottom line with this is DDR3 is the fastest. Just remember that on the exam. Understand the minor differences between the other ones. This is just memorization territory. You should do fine on DRAM types on the exam.

RAM CHARACTERISTICS

When we talk about RAM Characteristics what we're really talking about is the packaging, in the actual physical form that the RAM takes and, of course, we're also talking about its functionality and there are four basic types of memory packages or characteristics that you need to be aware of on this exam. You need to be able to recognize these visually and then you need to know just a minimal amount of information about their performance and then just a couple of little oddities about them.

Well, the four types, you can see the first one here - SIMM, that is, a Single Inline Memory Module. DIMM is a Dual Inline Memory Module. A SODIMM is a Small Outline Dual Inline Memory Module. And then, everybody's favorite, the MicroDIMM, the Micro Dual Inline Memory Module.

Now let's drill into each one of these and I just want to give you some visuals and talk about some basics. The Single Inline Memory Module is what we first saw in the original PCs and we watched them as

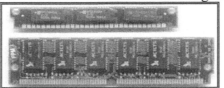

they grew through the late 90s even.

But a SIMM, a Single Inline Memory Module really means that, if you'll notice, these contacts on the bottom that plug into the motherboard, this thing basically had contacts on both sides but they were redundant, meaning that you only sent data, you know, through one path, but the path had contacts on both sides of the memory module. Now the early SIMMs were 30 pins like you see on the top picture, and it provided data in 8-bit data chunks. And later they became 72-pin, like this one on the bottom, the large one, and it provided data in 32-bit data chunks which obviously meant this one was a lot faster, it can move a lot more information because it was moving larger chunks. It's the same thing as having a larger bucket to haul water in. You can move a lot more water in a larger bucket.

Now, let's talk about SIMMs just a moment here. SIMMs had an issue and when our computers were growing and we're moving from 8-bit to 16-bit to 32-bit to 64-bit data paths, we had a challenge here and that is that the number of SIMMs that are required to fill the data path of the processor is called the Memory Bank. And let's think about this. If we have a 32-bit processor path, in other words, the processor is moving data back and forth to the memory in 32-bit chunks, then we need 32 bits of receptacles out there, if you will, on the RAM. I hope this makes sense.

But if our processor's communicating to us on 32 bits we have to be able to catch 32 bits on the RAM and deliver it. And so with a SIMM, if we were using the 30-pin 8 bit RAM chips then we'd have to have four of them because 4 times 8 equals 32. We're back to that third grade math that you used to wonder when you'd ever use that in real life. Or, if you have a 32-bit path then you could just use one of the 72-pin, 32 bit SIMMs, but again, we had to make sure that the data path coming off the processor matched up with our SIMM memory chips. The Pentium systems went to 64 bit which now meant that you had to have two 72-pin 32 bit SIMMS and, of course, 2 times 32 equals the 64 bits and so we could work.

Now the world of the DIMM changed a few things, not a lot. A Dual Inline Memory Module - it's the same as the SIMM but it delivered the data in 64-bit chunks. One of the main ways it did it was the

little contacts that are on both sides here were unique on both sides, which meant you had twice as many contacts, more or less, and so our data width doubled from 32 to 64 bit. Your original DIMMs were 168 and, again, you'll notice in most techs recognized RAM based on the size of the chip, the age of the computer, and the number of breaks or where the breaks are on the bottom on these. They're all unique. So the original DIMMs were 168 pin.

The DDR DIMMs you see here  are 184. Notice the breaks in a different place and there's only one. DDR2 and DDR3 DIMMs are 240 pins. And DIMMs are the most popular type in use today, so watch for that on the exam. If you're looking at memory in most computers today the characteristic or the layout or the type, whatever you want to call it, is going to be a DIMM, Dual Inline Memory Module.

SODIMMS are Small Outline DIMMs and these are used in laptops and you may have seen these if you've ever worked with RAM in a laptop. The 32-bit SODIMMS have 72 pins and this is what they look like. The 64-bit SODIMMs have 144 pins. This is what they look like

. Notice the little break almost in the middle. And then the 200 64-bit pins which happen to be DDR and DDR2 type memory looks like this and you will notice here, again, the little break. It looks like about the first fourth of the memory module in the bottom on the physical layout. So that's SODIMM.

Now MicroDIMM is also used in laptops and it really is the same as SODIMM, it's just again, smaller

. There's a 144-pin for SDRAM type memory. There's 172-pin model for the DDR-type memory. And so that's your basic RAM Characteristics and types. Just be generally familiar with these. Make sure that you understand which ones are used when the data bits, the pin numbers and then again, to be able to recognize them by looking at them and you will be able to figure out the answers on the A+ Exam.

PC PROCESSORS

Now let's step inside the box, if you will, and let's take a look at the Processor because there are a lot of things about a Processor that you need to understand in the real world and you need to have an understanding of to pass the A+ Exam because they're going to drill into this quite a bit. So let's just start off with the basic what is a Processor and then we'll talk about some things you need to know about it and then we'll spend quite a few sections or chapters talking about various aspects and characteristics of the Processor that you need to be aware of.

First of all, the Processor is the CPU and that stands for Central Processing Unit, and you will hear all of those terms interchanged. You will hear people call it the Processor, the CPU, the Processing Unit, the Central Processor, all those things mean the same thing. The bottom line, this is the brain of your computer. It performs, organizes and controls most of the processing that takes place when you're using your compute, and notice I said most of the processing. Because as it became the bottleneck as the computer was evolving and getting more powerful, we found ways to start to offload things from the Processor, and these are still considered functionalities of the Processor but they're offloaded, and we're talking things like Level 2 Cache, and that sort of thing, and so we will talk about those in separate sections.

But, for the most part, the Processor is the control area, the bridge of the Enterprise, if you will. On the bridge, if you'll remember in Star Trek, it's not that they did everything on the bridge, but everything was coordinated through there and everything involved instructions from the bridge. Now this is a picture

of a motherboard. Now if you open your computer and look at it yours will not look this neat and clean.

But anyways, there are no connections going on here, but if you will notice, this is the CPU. Now there's not a CPU on here right now, this is actually, it looks like an open socket, but this is where you will see the CPU and it is generally the most predominant piece of equipment on the motherboard. And if you will notice, it tends to be kind of centrally located. We'll talk about what all these other pieces and parts are a little bit later on in the course, but I wanted you to see.

Now I want to strongly encourage you as you go through this course to occasionally take the side or the back off of your PC and just look at it. If it's plugged up don't stick your hands in there. I would strongly recommend you unplug it before you take the sides or the back off, but just go in there and kind of look around, and you will see these various pieces and parts.

Also, if you know someone who is in an IT department, especially at a large company, or a training company, if you have a local training company that you've ever used, just go ask their local nerds for, say, have you got any old motherboards I can have? Trust me. They have plenty of them that have cracked, that have shorted out, that don't work anymore, and they just hadn't thrown them away yet. Grab one of these and take it home and use it to help yourself prepare because this is something you can play with, you can practice inserting RAM and cards in, you don't have to worry about breaking the thing. Ask them if they have some old cards and even some old CPUs that you can practice inserting these. It'll really help you when you get out there in the real world.

Now, the things that you need to know for the A+ Exam about the Processor, I'm just going to list them here so that you don't get confused when you see all the sections that you're going to see here, and I want you to know that these are directly related to the Processors. You need to understand the popular Processors that are out on the market because these are the stepping stones that we've used to get to where we are with our current technologies. The speed of the Processors - how do we manage or, not manage and, in some cases, yes manage, but more importantly, how do we rate these Processors and how does that actually affect the computer itself and the speed in which it runs.

The Data Bus, we'll talk about what the Data Bus is, how important that is to performance along with the Processor. The Address Bus, same thing. We'll talk about the Registers on the Processor, how that affects it. Cache Memory, the Math Co-Processor, whether your Processor runs in real mode or protected mode and how that affects how your computer behaves and responds.

MMX, this is somewhat of, most people would consider this an old technology but in reality it's still here. We'll talk about what it is. You will get asked about MMX a lot of times on the exam. It's still a favorite type question. Hyper threading, Multicore, which is one of the hot things now, we'll talk about it in a separate section, Throttling the Processor, Overclocking the Processor, we're talking about speeding it up, slowing it down. And then Chip Packaging, which is kind of how the Processor is put together and the basic architecture of it. So, as you can see, there's a lot of things to be concerned with the Processor and so there's the list. So, watch for these sections coming up later on in the course so that you'll understand that there's a lot going on with the Processor that you need to understand. It's not complicated, it's all very logical and we're just going to step through them one at a time and get you where you need to be.

PROCESSOR SPEEDS

The speed of the Processor or the CPU has kind of come to be known as the one major factor that we consider when we're looking at the strength of a Processor and when we're trying to determine the overall efficiency and speed of the computer. This is not necessarily so, and you need to understand this and you need to understand how the Processor speed works in preparation for this exam.

The first thing to understand is that the Processor speed is measured in the number of instructions per second that the Processor can process. And these are measured in what's called Megahertz, and you'll notice capital M, capital H lowercase z. Now, megahertz is millions of instructions per second and obviously that's pretty quick so in English that means that if a Processor's rated at 1 megahertz then it can carry out one million tasks every second.

Now keep in mind that the first CPUs that came out on those early IBM 3270 PCs and on even on the early, the first version of the Apple Macintosh ran at 4.77 megahertz or basically 4.7 million instructions per second, and of course, nowadays we're measuring our Processors in gigabits per second, or GHz, and that is billions of instructions per second and to quote Steve Jobs, that's billions with a B. Now, keep in mind when you look at a computer in the real world and once you've passed your A+ and you're out there as a technician that the Processor speed or the rated megahertz or gigahertz is only one aspect of system performance.

Now, generally, the faster the Processor speed the faster the computer, but there are other things that will greatly affect that and you also need to be aware that the speed of the Processor can be adjusted under various conditions, and from a troubleshooting standpoint you need to keep this in mind and we will talk about that a lot more in a section entitled **Speeding Up and Slowing Down**, and you can find that section somewhere else in the course, so we'll kind of skip over that for now and I'll just refer you to Speeding Up and Slowing Down to go a little deeper there.

Now, when we're talking about the Processor speed what we're really talking about on a technical level is something called Clock Speed because if you'll think about what a Processor is doing it's getting requests kind of through something called interrupts but it's getting requests from everybody - the user types on the keyboard and the keyboard tries to tell the Processor I got instructions coming in. The user moves the mouse and the mouse tells the Processor, hey, I've got some instructions coming in. The hard disk, we're requested some information, it's sending information back, and it's telling the Processor, hey, I've got some information coming in. So what the Clock Speed on the Processor does is it really kind of serves as the drummer for the PC band, so just think of everything under the hood on that PC as a band and if any of you guys reading this have ever been in a band or if you've ever worked in music, this is really the beat of the music. This keeps everybody in sync, and so the CPU now knows when instructions start and when they stop and really, again, back to music here, if it's a 4-4 beat, one, two, three, four, one, two, three, four, we know that one is the beginning of every measure and four is the end of that measure.

Well, in CPU language, from one to four, one, two, three, and four would be part of one instruction and when we start back over at one that's a new instruction, so this is a method, the Clock Speed, is a way for the CPU to know when one task is completed and another one is starting up. And there is a clock wire on the bus, we'll talk about buses later, that transmit begin and end messages. And so, really what's going on here is that the Clock Speed or the real speed of that Processor, the effective speed, determines the maximum number of instructions over a particular given period of time. And what I find fascinating is in the manufacturing process, take Intel. Intel builds every Processor that they're building to run at the maximum Processor speed. Maybe it's 3.0 Gigahertz, but when they pull some of the Processors off and test them, connection, manufacturing issues, whatever, it can only actually efficiently operate without errors at say 2.8. Well, guess what? That gets tagged as a 2.8 Processor and put in the machine.

So, all of our Processors are basically running at their maximum stretch, but just keep in mind that the Clock Speed is the drummer for the PC band. It determines the stop and start places for every individual instruction and the number of times, the number of measures, or individual instructions it can do in a second. It's going to be rated in Megahertz, millions of instructions per seconds, or Gigahertz, a billion instructions per second. And just keep in mind this drummer for the PC band, and this drummer is not necessarily there to make it get faster and louder all the time, OK? This one keeps it totally in sync and it keeps everybody looking at the same instruction step, so there's some rough information, some quick information on the Processor speed. This should help you understand how to get through the questions that you're going to see about Processor speed on the A+ Exam.